BOOK 3

MOVIE & TV HITS for TEENS

9 GRADED SELECTIONS
FOR LATE INTERMEDIATE PIANISTS

ARRANGED BY DAN COATES

The *Movie & TV Hits for Teens* series presents carefully leveled, accessible arrangements for the teenage pianist. This series provides students with the opportunity to develop their technique and musicianship while performing popular pieces from their favorite movies and television shows.

CONTENTS

Produced by
Alfred Music
P.O. Box 10003
Van Nuys, CA 91410-0003
alfred.com

Printed in USA.

ISBN-10: 1-4706-3806-1
ISBN-13: 978-1-4706-3806-1

Cover art:
Young people in theater: © Getty Images / izusek • Woman at the cinema: © Getty Images / andresr • Popcorn: © Getty Images / ktsimage •
Film industry icons: © Getty Images / lushik • Cinema concept design: © Getty Images / sgursozlu • Banners: © Getty Images / traffic_analyzer

DOWNTON ABBEY: THE SUITE

(from *Downton Abbey*)

Composed by John Lunn
Arr. Dan Coates

DOCTOR WHO
(Main Theme)

By Ron Grainer
Arr. Dan Coates

THE FASTEST MAN ALIVE

(from the television series *The Flash*)

Composed by Blake Neely
Arr. Dan Coates

FRIEND LIKE ME

(from Walt Disney's *Aladdin*)

Words by Tim Rice
Music by Alan Menken
Arr. Dan Coates

brand of mag - ic nev - er fails. ____ You got some ____ And I'll ____ say,
got - ta do is rub that lamp. ____

_f_ Mis - ter A - lad - din sir, ____ what will your pleas - ure be?

Let me take your or - der, jot it down. You ain't

nev - er had a friend like me. No, no, ____ no. Life is your

res - tau - rant ____ and I'm your maî - tre d'. ____ C' - mon,

FLICKER
(Kanye West Rework)
(from *The Hunger Games: Mockingjay Part 1*)

Words and Music by Mike Dean,
Ella Yelich-O'Connor, Noah D Goldstein and Kanye West
Arr. Dan Coates

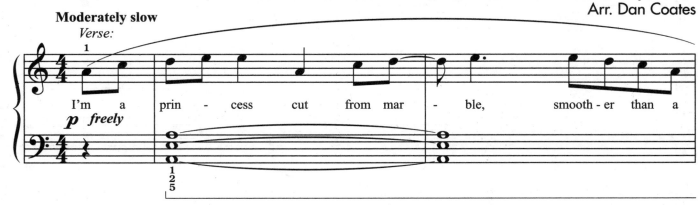

HEATHENS

(from *Suicide Squad*)

Words and Music by Tyler Joseph
Arr. Dan Coates

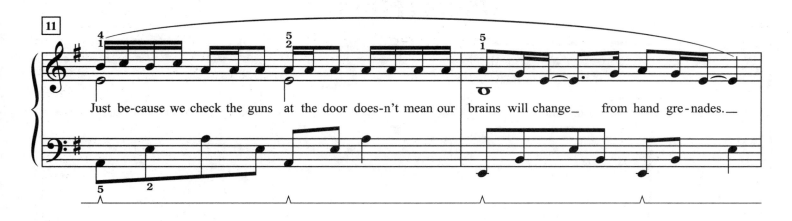

Just be-cause we check the guns at the door does-n't mean our brains will change_ from hand gre-nades._

You lov-in' on the psy-cho-path sit-ting next to you. You lov-in' on the mur-der-er sit-ting next to

you. You'll think, "How'd I get here, sit-ting next to you?" But af-ter all I've said,

please don't for-get. All my friends are hea-thens, take it slow.

Chorus:

mf

Wait for them to ask you who you know. Please don't make an - y sud - den

moves.___ You don't know the half of the a - buse.___

Verse:

We don't deal with out - sid - ers ver - y well. They say new - com - ers have a cer - tain smell.

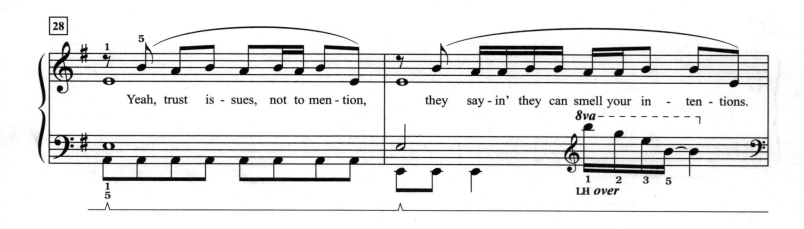

Yeah, trust is - sues, not to men - tion, they say - in' they can smell your in - ten - tions.

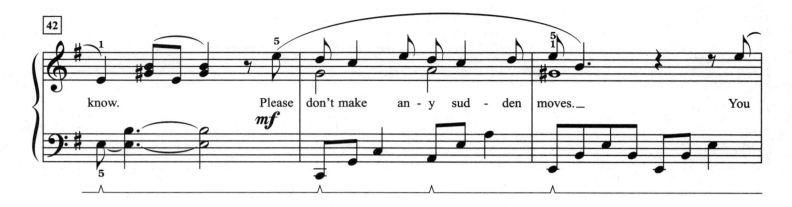

know.   Please don't make an-y sud-den moves.___   You

don't know the half of the a - buse._____   Why'd you come, you knew you should have

stayed.   I tried to warn you just to stay a - way.   And

now they're out-side read-y to bust.   It looks like you might be one of us.

NOT TODAY

(from *Me Before You*)

Words and Music by Michael Daly, Benjamin McKee,
Daniel Platzman, Daniel Reynolds and Daniel Sermon
Arr. Dan Coates

STAR WARS
(Main Theme)

Music by **JOHN WILLIAMS**
Arr. Dan Coates

OVER THE RAINBOW

(from *The Wizard of Oz*)

Music by Harold Arlen
Lyrics by E.Y. Harburg
Arr. Dan Coates